A TASTE OF

Childr
Short Stories

Nicole d'Altena

Written, Edited and Published

by Nicole d'Altena 2024

with the great support and contribution

of Lucy Ambrose

◊

Printed in the UK in 2024

by TJ Books

◊

ISBN 978-1-917010-33-7

◊

...why not create your own drawings

imagined from the stories?

...or play them...

...ENJOY!..

◊

The right of Nicole d'Altena to be identified as writer/publisher of this work has been asserted by her in accordance with the Copyright, Designs and Patents Acts 1988.

All rights reserved. No part of this book may be reproduced, transmitted, or stored in an information retrieval system in any form or by any means, graphic, electronic or mechanical, including photocopying, taping and recording, without prior written permission from the author.

This book is a work of memories and fiction, invented words, names, characters, places and events are products either of the author's imagination or are used fictitiously.

Many thanks Brenda Barratt for your exquisite drawings, Jade Osborne for her charming contribution of drawings, Jacqui Bennett for your invaluable computer knowledge, Robert and Shawn Lowe, Lucy

Ambrose and it goes without saying Pamela Osborne who helped me with the revisions and edits. I couldn't have made it without your inestimable skills as well as all the other friends who helped me!

This book also gets distributed to charities.

The author's mother tongues are Englishish, Frenchish and Italianish and many words in Espanish. Any made up words, written sounds, and quirky grammar are deliberate and are just part of the joy of her books.

www.destinitybooks.com

CONTENTS

LIFE IS LIKE A KITE	page 4
THAT INVISIBLE SOMETHING	page 8
MATHEMATICAL ALPHABET OF JAN AND JOHN'S STORY	page 7
A LIVING WAY	page 9
THE ODD AND THE EVEN	page 11
THE SPACE ADVENTURER	page 12
THE INVENTOR OF WORDS	page 14
WELL DONE LUCKY WORM	page 17
THE MOON STORYTELLER	page 20
PARADISE... AND AFTER	page 24
THE ATYPICAL WAY	page 35

◊ LIFE IS LIKE A KITE ◊

The kite lies on the ground with an imperceptible shiver at first. Once awakened, the kite gets prepared while deeply thinking about flying.

With phases of total self-assurance, other times shy or with hesitations, it finally makes its mind up and ZOOM, up it goes and starts flying. Sometimes, to begin, it struggles to take off.

But, in time, it manages and carries on uplifting and winding with twists and turns, diving up and diving down and around in all directions, like contortionists do.

Eventually, the kite manages to stabilise itself for a short while
before it carries on.

At times, the rain comes and soaks the kite. The wind can blow pretty harshly as well, not to mention those angry thunderstorms.

Occasionally, it gets in deep trouble when stuck like in a tree in a very awkward and uneasy position. It struggles to release itself and glide freely again.

Before reaching the sky, the kite dances incessantly, avoiding obstacles, executing spectacular and daring jumps, somersaults, and acrobatics.

It hovers for a while and, should the wind dare rest, the kite automatically subsides and falls quickly back to the ground where it all started!

...The kite lies on the ground...
After a while, the kite comes back to life with an imperceptible shiver at first.

Once awakened, the dynamics of this game takes off once more, and the kite starts flying all over again for the story to continue.

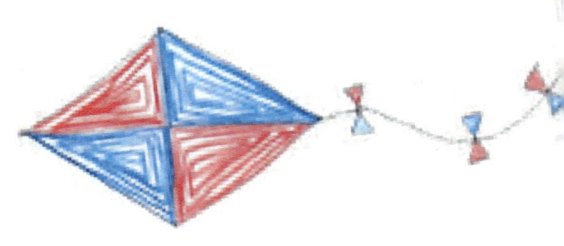

◊ THAT INVISIBLE SOMETHING ◊

There was a child imprisoned in an ice-coated castle.

She had to serve an atrociously horrible Ogre. That child didn't get eaten because the Ogre needed a servant.

Fortunately, sometimes the Ogre would fall into a deep sleep to digest his food, after eating like a pig and drinking like a fish.

When this happened, the child had plenty of spare time to look out of the window. She would get drawn out into the air and would start to fly.

At first, she didn't fly for long and she often fell to the ground. But, determined as ever, she would gather all her energy to make herself run as fast as she could to take off again and again.

She practiced flying as much as she could before she was sucked back inside the cold castle to serve this nasty Ogre. She loathed serving the Ogre intensely.

At each flying practice she became better and better. The first time she flew low but, as time went by, she went higher and higher and wider and wider, gradually she discovered the marvels of nature.

At every attempt, she pushed herself further and further. Many times, she'd have vertigo and get dizzy, lightheaded. It could be pretty scary sometimes, but it was also so thrilling!

She wasn't aware that during her training there was an 'Invisible Something' looking at her with amazement and admiration.

"Gee, how do you do that? It looks so great!" the 'Invisible Something' said one day. The child looked over her shoulder, turned around and then looked all over again. Though she couldn't see anything, she didn't feel threatened and came to the conclusion that it was something invisible, supportive and friendly.

The child replied with a shining, happy and excited smile while she was flying: "I don't know, I just do it, I cannot explain it. But one thing for sure', when I'll be good at it, I shall fly away forever."

And when that time came the 'Invisible Something' flew away with her.

◊ MATHEMATICAL ALPHABET
OF JAN AND JOHN'S STORY ◊

A story has an ending which can be happy or sad, but it always rests on the ending and there could be many endings in the same story.

'A' & 'A' - Jan and John - were childhood sweethearts. Everyone thought they'd be together forever. And that would be the ending of a very short story indeed...
...but it carries on.

'A' - Jan - went up Country.
'A' - John - went sailing around the world.
Life kept on turning 24 hours a day and...
'A' & 'A' - Jan and John - were caught in Life's pace.

They changed; they split up and finally lost touch.

She became 'B' – Jan. He became 'C' – John.
'B' - Jan - studied to experience lots of culture and became very knowledgeable. It led her to have a responsible career.

'C' - John - learnt plenty of things through his experiences and travels, and most of the time, he had a lot of fun. Circumstances of life, as they often do, made that:

'B' - Jan - got married and had two children.
'C' - John - got married and had one, too.
'B' - Jan - went through her adventures of life. 'C' - John - went through his too.
As for all people, their events and experiences were unique.

Jan's story with her husband and John's story with his wife didn't work out.
B' – Jan - returned to her roots.
Jan and John were together once more!
They became 'E' & 'E'.
And that could be the ending of a middle length story...

If it ends now, it will have one connotation, but if this story continues it would have another.

Do you want to know how it carried on?
Well... they entered many of life's adventures but, eventually, they gave up being a couple once more.

'E' became 'F' – Jan -
'E' became 'G' – John –

There's more...

Don't get upset now! They really remained very good friends.

Now they are retired; they travel a lot, they are always together, they have real great fun discovering the world and they play very often at all sorts of pleasurable activities. And now, it's the end of the story.

◊ A LIVING WAY ◊

If you wish to function well in life, your body must be well cared for: it's your life's vehicle.
Good vehicle = good chances.
Bad vehicle = bad life.
No vehicle = no life.

It's like maintaining a car: if you take good care of your car, it will be in good condition and very pleasant to drive, if you don't, be well warned you will regret it, that's absolutely certain! But then it will be too late...

Naturally, Destiny is involved... but no one has control or a say over that!

* * *

BODY: take good care of your body. Be physical and active, maintain suppleness.

Examples: exercising, walking, running, dancing, yoga.

WEIGHT: to keep fit and maintain your body in good running order.
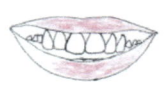
Eat balanced healthy foods, drink water, only drink alcohol sparingly and never go for fizzy beverages with added sugar and chemicals, etc...

TEETH: take good care of your teeth.
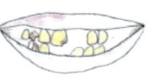
Clean your teeth morning and night to stop the decay and rot of your teeth. Don't ruin them by eating wrong foods like sugar, or using your teeth to cut things or as bottle openers, etc...

SKIN: take care of your skin. Keep out of the sun and beware of chemicals. Use sun creams and screens to

protect yourself from sunrays, don't stay in the sun all day; it can be dangerous! etc... We have got 5 senses. They are precious gifts. Be warned, take good care of them, they can never be replaced:

Hearing – Tasting – Smelling – Seeing – Touching

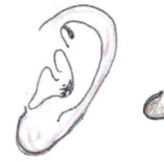

HEARING: be careful not to become deaf by negligence, use ear protectors for loud noises, like concerts, noisy tools, insects, etc.

TASTING: protect yourself from losing your sense of smell and taste, avoid eating too hot, too salty or too acid food, etc...

SMELLING: protect yourself from losing your sense of taste and smell, avoid dust and offensive smells, always wear a mask if you work near chemicals or fibres, like ceramic makers or carpenters do, etc...

SEEING: protect your eyes from sunrays, from chemicals, dust, fiberglass and smoke, etc... Wear spectacles if needed and, later in life, have your eyesight regularly checked.

Expressions:
'It 'it goes without saying' - one can use that expression in so many situations. It's amazing how it can get one out tactfully and with skill from impossible, awkward, or difficult situations without having to commit oneself.

'I'll think about it' and 'I'll bear it in mind' will allow you to have enough space and time to think and analyse before answering!
'BALANCE' and 'PRIORITIES' are maybe among the most important words to know. Think about it.

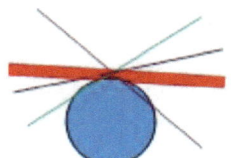

Never, ever forget that facts are stubborn!
Be informed and never take things for granted.

Be mindful, take time out to be in silence, the fruits are uncountable!

One learns more by observing, seeing and listening, though sometimes talking is also necessary, and in some cases, indispensable!

Be attentive to this advice; it is very important! You could avoid many painful health complications later in life.
There! You'll never be able to say that you haven't been fully warned and informed!

Have a good life!

◊ THE ODD and THE EVEN ◊

One day, in outer space, there was an odd and an even who inadvertently bumped into each other.

Eventually one of the two suggested, in Galaxy's language, to go to the close-by Seven Star Pub. This wouldn't take long to reach, merely a few mega miles from where they were standing.

The odd said: "do you realize that we are better than you evens because adding an odd to an even will always produce an odd ".

The even became infuriated and retorted: "not so! We are the best because if you added an even to an even or an odd to an odd it will always result in an even."

After which, the odd became yet more arrogant and said "but you do admit that you did have the need of an odd?
"I do" said the even with a sneaky smile, "but you'd have to admit as well that you needed an even to make an odd!"

The tone was gradually becoming louder. Someone had to have the last word and inevitably win! Evidently, someone had to give in!

Who was going to win in the end, the odd or the even?

Whatever they said, they were both completely befuddled by now, and anyway, it didn't really matter in the slightest, it was of no importance whatsoever for the time being.

They both agreed and laughed, and had another yummy, quirky, sparkling drink. They mutually agreed that it made them 'odd ' sorry 'even '... he- he... correction, it made them 'EQUAL'.

They carried on giggling and mingling together forever after, conceiving further infinite off-shoots of unlimited numbers.

◊ THE SPACE ADVENTURER ◊

Coming from the far pink-blue horizon, was a man riding a computerised, tall, well-behaved and obedient donkey; that is as close as it could be described... latest model if you please!

He was galloping in the direction of the Pub, trailing huge high clouds of sprinkling dust, not surprisingly called 'traveling dust'.

The rider, (when exploring, more than a Pub that is), wore a handsome Cowboy-style coat that shimmered at a distance.

Inside the rider's long coat were embedded many screens of all different sizes and shapes functioning in a military disciplined mode.

He was a SPACE ADVENTURER! A pioneer, one might say! He was investigating the cosmos close by his home planet, Planet Earth.

His skin was ruffled more than the meaning of the word ruffled.

His long journey meant he was very hungry and thirsty. He was dehydrated and famished. He urgently needed solid and liquid refuelling. It was long time overdue! He was seeking balanced food and energising beverages to absorb thoroughly so that he could continue his expedition in full form and safely.

He stopped at the Pub, with his reliable donkey.

While sipping his first drink, he casually asked at the counter: "Oh, by the way, just out of curiosity, is pollution and unfriendly waste in the Cosmos Territory on the agenda as well, like it is drastically on Planet Earth?"
"Do you have comparable dire problems we are experiencing on Planet Earth with the

Worldwide Plague of Plastic on Land and in the Sea which is on the verge of eradicating civilization?!"

"Does Dyslexia, with sometimes its numerous qualities and advantages, also exist in the Cosmos?"
"What other similar problems to Planet Earth do you have?"
"And what about the score of good coffee shops in the Universe?"

It was part of his 1,000 long list of unanswered questions he was seeking to solve.
Coincidentally, he had also overheard from afar the conversation a couple were having.
He was amazed, he was!

Then, analysing and scrutinising scientifically at long length with his indispensable, pleasant, well-behaved, and obedient, reliable, computerized tall donkey, he finally made a long deep approving "hmmmm" sound and commented:

"One can hear very similar exchanges down on Planet Earth! We are not so different after all!

◊ THE INVENTOR OF WORDS ◊

There are many stories about Inventors of Words, here's one of them:

There once was a place where all kinds of people would come and meet. It was called the 'Café des Importants'.

They all seemed, in their own right, quite fascinating:

Some were angry with the government, some criticising greatly and wanting to change the world without even moving out of their chair.

Some oblivious to reality, preferring to talk about art with great pretentiousness, feigning to speak with immense knowledge. Some were just utterly bonkers.

One thing for sure they all felt 'very important'.

This little world, which was like a big family, gathered daily in this 'Café des Importants'. It was their place, their habitat, their home: it felt safe. Depending on how one looked at them one could call them 'mighty boring'! Their exchanges were so well rehearsed that, as time passed by, their retorts became totally expected.

They eventually ran out of words.
Why did they bother to carry on talking?

Rarely this stew would get interrupted, yet unexpectedly, one day, a stranger walked into this 'Café des Importants'.

The noise fell silent for just for a few seconds, then the crowd soon turned their backs to him. They were clinging on to their habits of great importance and pride which they never wanted to have disrupted.

The stranger went to the counter and ordered a drink which was served to him with a slight weary hesitation.
Whilst he was drinking, he turned to look around to gage what was happening in in this noisy and grotty place.

"Who are you?" said a voice.
It was a young man, sitting next to him. The latest addition to become part of this stagnant crowd.

He was green enough for his mind not to have completely seized up and to fortunately have remained still quite curious.

"I", said the stranger with majesty, as if he was standing on a stage, looking at the crowd head high from the corner of his eyes, "am an Inventor of Words".

"How can you claim that?" promptly exclaimed the young man, "it doesn't exist!" "Who says?" exclaimed the Inventor of Words with an extraordinarily deep voice.

The Inventor's dark emerald eyes went silent and half closed, looking up in the sky for new inspirations.

As soon as he had invented a new word, the word became multi-coloured and very bright.

"Here's one, it's for you, it's a gift!" said the Inventor, whispering in the young man's ear his newly invented word.

"Oh, what a nice word!" replied the young man.

The word melted in his teeth and softened nearly like jelly on the surface of his tongue. He was tasting the word and rolling it in his mouth on a dynamic tune and an attractive perfume was emanating in mid-air.

"It's a little bit like music, it bounces and bubbles, it's happy and soothing and as soft as velvet. It has so many qualities, it's hard to describe and with such a nice sound!

"What is its significance?!" asked the young man.
"Whatever you want it to mean", said the Inventor, "that's the beauty you get when you are an Inventor of Words... there are no rules!"
"Anyone can become an Inventor of Words... it only depends on wanting to be one...
...the numbers of words are unlimited... and you can go even further... you can mix up expressions, modify their combinations, have a variety of languages bunched all together...

...you can even add squeezes of sounds or make delectable cocktails with them...
...you also could create them to resemble fireworks...
...you can make anything you want out of words...
...everything is possible, except for a few rules in grammar which handles the circuits of understanding, but that's OK because they allow things not to become too hectic."
"Wahoo! exclaimed the young man, smiling up to his ears and twinkling eyes, "this is really cool, I'm getting out of here!"

"Hey! Thanks for the tip!" and he walked out without even finishing his drink.

He left to the past what belonged to the past and, at a distance, one could hear him joyfully whistling.

When, every now and then, the young man would stop, it meant he'd just invented another word.

The Inventor of Words, disappeared... He was the Magician of Words.

◊ WELL DONE, LUCKY WORM! ◊

This story is based on a true story.

It was an especially beautiful day that day and all day through.

There was a big, fat, juicy Worm who had a lot of fun and plenty to eat, his body was bursting full.

The Sun finally decided that it had done enough shining and started to turn off the lights and go to bed.

The Worm was also getting tired; he had had another busy day playing.

So, just before the dusk turned to darkness, the Worm stood up on all his legs to head home.

There was a little road to cross which the Worm always feared but it had to be done.

It was a very small little road for us human beings, nonetheless, for a Worm, even a fat and juicy one, it was equal to cross over a four-lane busy motorway, which is always extremely dangerous even with little traffic.

The Worm was really looking forward to lying down in its cuddly bed, which shouldn't take too long now.

So here it is going back home, surrounded by flowers, stroked by fresh grass and sometimes tickled by earth rubbing his belly.

Eventually, the Worm reached the edge of this big obstacle; the motorway, this 'wretched little road' for us and a 'big one' for him.

Just as the Worm had begun to tackle this dangerous ordeal, suddenly, out of nowhere, appeared a little Bird! It had been happily flying and couldn't believe its eyes when it saw such a big Worm.

That's because, on a road, whatever its size, there's no hiding!

The little Bird shot the Worm just like an arrow would and, seconds later, the destiny of the Worm changed radically. It seemed like no more cuddly beds and good food for it ever again. It was the Worm's turn to be transformed into a nice meal for the little Bird, nice because it was so juicy.

To the Spirits that were looking at this fascinating scene, much to their dismay, the story didn't end there.

The Worm was held tightly in the beak of the little Bird, but it wasn't yet dead. It was kept alive, one supposed, the meat had to be kept fresh for the little Bird's babies.

You see, the reason why the story continued, is because the little Bird was totally unaware, that just as it became like an arrow, higher above, a Magpie was flying, who guessed instantly what was going to happen.

As the law of nature goes, the Magpie went for the Worm too, but it arrived at the scene fractions too late to catch the bait. It was flying so powerfully that it couldn't break.

The Magpie was very greedy, and all this situation made it extremely frustrated and terribly angry and, just as the little Bird caught the fat Worm, the Magpie flew by and hit violently the little Bird's head.

While the little Bird was struck into an instant shock, the Worm still couldn't figure out what had happened to him, but 'something definitely wasn't quite right' and it was very frightened; it all went far too quick!

Well, one of them had to win.

The Magpie lost, though the little bird remained in shock and had become like a shivering statue, still holding on tightly and without killing this traumatised big fat Worm.

It's as if it was all arranged for this to happen, because a car arrived just at the right moment and stopped to witness this scene.

The car driver had just received very bad news and was in great sorrow, but when she saw the little Bird's misfortune, the car driver forgot how much she was shattered and hurting.

"You're going to be OK" she said, "you're just in shock!" and without thinking she took the little Bird under her wings.

After spending a long time calming down the little Bird and telling it that everything was going to be alright, she took it to the Vet to be nursed and for a good dose of Psychotherapy.

The first thing the little Bird had to do was to 'let go of the Worm', much to its enormous relief. It was heavily bruised and had quite a few deepcuts.

Though thoroughly shaken, the Worm was all right and, a while later, was released and put in a garden which surprisingly enough happened to be very close to its home.

It didn't have to cross that wretched little road for us, a 'big one' for the Worm.

It arrived home knackered at dawn, just as the Sun was preparing itself for another newly born day and to shine without interruption until it was ready to go back to sleep again.

The Worm was too tired, it had lived a 'real close one' and was startled to have survived! It decided to skip playing for 24 hours and, without hesitation, it went straight to bed.

That day, its bed was the most comfortable and cuddly bed in the world.

And if there had to be a moral to this story, certainly it would be to never take things for granted!

◊ THE MOON STORYTELLER ◊

This is a story which some parents would have liked to have been told when they were themselves children and didn't like to go to bed and sleep.

Once upon a time, there was a child who never liked going to bed since he couldn't get to sleep.

His parents were very distressed about this problem because, other than that, he was a very good little child.

So, they went to see a specialist doctor who said what he needed was a sweet remedy for sleeping problems, and this was to tell a very special story to the child.

When the night arrived, down came the Moon Storyteller: "Who are you?" said the child.

"I am the Moon Storyteller. I live on the Moon when night-time falls on your planet."
"Never!" said the child incredulously, "that can't be true!"

"Oh! yes, it is only a matter of closing your eyes and believing it. I tell you what, I'll wave at you tonight from up there, will you wave back?"

"Okay," said the child, dubious and still not quite convinced.

The next evening the Moon Storyteller came back to the child's bedside.

"Did you see me last night; I was waving at you?"
"Oh yes, said the child, I did, did you see me wave too?"
"Of course I did!" answered the Moon Storyteller with a big smile,
while preparing himself to leave.

"Oh, don't go away," said the child, "I can't go to sleep, it's hard, it's so difficult!"
"What do you mean, you can't go to sleep? You don't know what you are missing! You can even go to the Moon if you wanted to!"
"Really?" said the child, "never! that can't be true."
"Yes, it is true, really! It is only a matter of closing your eyes and believing it."

So, the child closed his eyes tightly, though he was quite sceptical about this, but soon he sensed, as he was melting into his bed and becoming lighter and lighter, and being lifted up and up......and la-la-la round and round and round la-la-la-la-la......until he reached the Moon.

The stars, which looked like dotted glittering spots from Planet Earth, were so very different in the Universe. They were all shapes and sizes and with colours never seen down here on Planet Earth.

The voyage didn't take too long, just several fractos, which is how they measure time on the Moon.

The Moon was majestically dressed in a silver cloak splattered with flickers of gold.

The child arrived not far from where the Moon Storyteller was standing.

"Hey! there, welcome, this is where I live."
"Wow! Wahoo!" said the child.
"When it is night on your Planet, the Moon can beam such a bright shining light on it, throughout the night, awaiting dawn and even at the beginning of the day sometimes, before disappearing."

Everything was so unfamiliar on the Moon; there were no words to describe it. One could only describe it when dreaming.

They spent several sub-fractos visiting the Planet. There was a lot to visit but they managed to visit it all in good time.
They ate special things which only grew on the Moon and in mid-air, nothing comparable to down here on Planet Earth.

Then some Mooninies turned up and they all started dancing to some special music.
The ground was made of soft velvet in greens, browns, yellows, oranges and reds. They were many hills scattered everywhere of different colours, sizes and curves. There was a huge variety of plants, trees, animals and weird things which the child had never seen before.

There was rain and wind, seas and lakes, storms and bright weather, and even snow, a lot like here on Planet Earth although very different, it was difficult to explain...

One could only describe it when dreaming... One definitely had to go up there and see for oneself. It was just simply a matter of closing one's eyes and believing it.

They went to visit the King who was so very pleased to meet yet another little child who couldn't get to sleep at night on his planet.

A banquet was prepared for this special Guest of Honour with delicious foods which only grew on the Moon, and the desserts were just as outstanding; one wasn't ashamed to be very greedy because it was so good, it was impossible to be otherwise or to resist!

They danced to their heart's content, floating sometimes in mid-air and they played different games that made them laugh so much it brought happy tears to their eyes!

But fractos had passed, it was time to leave.

The child was really upset, he felt so torn between wanting to stay on this exhilarating Moon or returning to his familiar Planet.

The Moon Storyteller guessed at once what was happening, he had a long experience in seeing such distress.

"You don't need to be so sad," he said with a generous wide smile, "you can come back here whenever you want to. I'm always here when night-time comes on your planet."

Ohhh! The child felt so relieved! He didn't have to choose between the Moon and Planet Earth, it would have been so unbearable, and, before he knew it, the child ended up in his bed.

"Good morning my darling," said his mother, "you went asleep so quickly and you look so rested, what happened?"
"You will never believe it he replied."
But he didn't have time to tell her before the school bus appeared.

When he gathered around all his friends before school started, he said with eagerness: "you will never believe where I went last night".
"Come on, tell us, don't leave us in suspense like this!"
"I've been up to the Moon," he proudly announced, with a slight blush, looking at his friends one by one.

Their eyes popped out in amazement and curiosity: it sounded so exciting! "Never!" said the children, uncertain of what they had just heard.

"Oh yesss," he said convincingly shaking his head, "it's true, it's only a matter of closing your eyes and believing it."

That night, before going to bed, the child opened the window wide open and looked up to the Moon and waved to his friend the Moon Storyteller!

And then he went straight to bed, keenly, peacefully and serenely.

And was soon fast asleep.
...and la-la-la and round and round and round la- la-la-la-la...

◊ PARADISE... AND AFTER ◊

In memory of Fellini and of his splendid film "Amarcord" the story of his enchanting youth and in memory of Paradise and After...

This story is based on a child's notion of Paradise ...

Once upon a time there was a beautiful simple girl and a just as remarkable Prince. They instantly fell in love with each other the first time they met and stayed together ever since. Their love was so pure and intense that after they died their love became encapsulated in immortality with illimited powers of enormous love.

Centuries later on the eruption of the volcano Epomeo in 1303 in the Isle of Ischia the lovers had another mission to accomplish which was to go down to Earth and protect the people of the Paradise Island of Ischia.

On that Island existed a very a special secret hidden garden where one could see one of the most beautiful birds in the world the peacock.

One would regularly go there to top up ones inner peace and absorb the magic qualities of the place.

Ater the afternoon traditional siesta, between 2pm and 4pm, an extraterrestrial sweet, serene sound of someone singing like nobody had heard before filled the air.

This unforgettable pure limpid angel voice could be heard every day after the siesta. No one could stop for just an instant when the sound started. One would find oneself in another realm of reality from this voice.

This cosmostic sound came up from the illuminated skies. It lasted a second or a century one was floating on another cosmoslity another dimension of reality.

This is where the story started off, a little girl and a little boy on the Isle of Paradise.

There once was an English Mother and a European Father. They had a little Girl and a little Boy who started their life on a stunning southern Italian Island.

The father was an artist whilst the mother was lovingly taking care of the children. Because they didn't have much money it was the most affordable location they had found to live.

Simple, modest, healthy. How lucky they were!

If ever Paradise existed on Earth, for sure, it would be right there on that fabulous Island!
It was undeniably certified to be the 'Children's Paradise on Earth'..

There is a group 'that would be children for ever' and another group 'of grown-ups for ever'. It's clear, no?

The children never had a hint nor concept of growing up one day. They always believed in that, it was official and never to be doubted, nor questioned, it was irrevocable.

The temperature was warm all year round; winter was just a few degrees lower than in summer and it didn't last for very long.

In those early days no cars were to be found or so few it's not even worth mentioning! For transport? Just donkeys or scanty horses and three wheeled scooters ('motorinos')

The Island was utterly safe as all the people of the Village kept a sharp eye on each other's Children. They were assisted or reprimanded when needed or did whatever was required to be done. By being so young, the children only played with the Village Islanders children.

All the children who were below school age, which in Italy only starts at 6, were left loose and were authorized to live their childhood at the full without schooling, choirs and restrictions. Just live and play and be unreservedly spoiled rotten! They had practically all the power it seems!

The English mother, as all good Brits systematically do, always kept on speaking in English to her children. They were too young to get their English quite correct and invented their own way of speaking it. Their parents got quite accustomed to it and never corrected them or interfered.

They were quite smart; they became completely accustomed to the Children's strange language and never interfered: "The Children will have plenty of time later on to straighten out their English and speak it correctly one day."

Anyway, you'd have to know English to understand their mother's Italian!

* * *

Here's how it went, sort of;

"Did you have a nice day, my darling?" said the Mother to her little Boy.
"Oh yeas, I was very busy playing a lot. I wented to the beach to look for shellses in the sandses, but I got bordereded, there are too much of them", said the little Boy, lifting his arms in disgust.
"So, I went in back of the changing cabins full of colours and I diggedated in the sandeses and made it run through my handses to catch the losted buttons" "I collected a lot of them today, big ones and smallses and all different coulourses, I had so much more fun..."
"Then I ran to the beach to go talk to my secret stones that I fished under the sea with my new swankee flippers."

He was so proud and content to have won his serious discussion he had with his father. It dealt with a negotiation of flippers with his father; "if you buy me flippers like you did for my sister, I will swim" said the little boy extremely seriously...and he did! He swam like a little boy mermaid ever since.

* * *

Occasionally the children went hunting in deeper waters near to fish shells and also beautiful eye of Saint Lucy (Occhio di Santa Lucia) . The shells hid between the rocks near the end of the pier where the sea was a little deeper where the lighthouse was. Only the eldest of the children could swim so deep, the younger ones merely attempted but quickly gave up. It was like a ceremonial which didn't last too long. Still, it was a stimulating challenge. The spectacle of exalted joy from children when one would find one was a must to witness.

When it was Sergiolino who would find an eye he systematically and generously gave it to the little Girl and little Boy without hesitation.

The Father even brought one to mount on a silver ring intertwined with a filet of gold to give to the Children's Mother for marking an important event. They could have been extinct by now if they were not farmed now.

* * *

"After, I wented for a walk and sawed old Caterina. I helped her put eggses in her basket, and when it was fillded, Maria pulled it with a string up to the skises were they livedenated.

"Then I went to see Benvenuto and worked very hard to help him sell at his Deli (Salumeria) and he gaves me some chocolates and a 'gelato nice cream' from 'Bar Maria' next door to say thank you ('grazie') to me."

"After I licktinated the 'nice cream', I ran down to the beach and I strolled and seed Ilario and Quinquale was there. We killeded some bugs of different colours and buried them in a mountain of sandses and made crosses with 'nice cream' sticks and straw and putted them on top of the mountain and said a mass with a lot of Ave Marias he proudly said." What a nice adventure!!"

* * *

Children and other little friends went playing in Gennaro enormous garden which also included a vineyard and many varieties of fruit trees which were picked up and eaten on the spot with delight. Some other parts of the garden one could brilliantly hide because the garden resembled a jungle.

The father's property was surrounded by numerous terraced poor terraced buildings which encircled Gennaro's father's huge property. The entrance of his property was sober but noticeable ... One could feel the great importance of the person living in it. If someone was lucky enough to go inside, it was like entering another world! When one entered would find oneself in a realm of exquisite unique tranquility. At great expense all the chairs and sofas were covered with heavy clear plastics to reveal the expensive material they used to cover their furniture. Unfortunately, the plastic very quickly discolored and one couldn't appreciate the richness of the material anymore. There were also two peacocks to represent royalty together with chicken running freely and running all over ana a faithful cuddly middle aged loving dog offering cuddles galore to all...

The children played all sorts of stories in that garden including the Jesus story one".

* * *

The children never liked Benito, Gennaro's young brother, but to be fair sometimes the younger siblings had a bitter raw deal. That is most probably why he was always whining and complaining and never contributed positively in the group, NEVER!

To keep him silent they reluctantly granted him to play Ponte Pilatus even if they weren't quite sure who Ponte Pilatus was, but they suspected rightly or wrongly he wasn't a nice guy.

It was only to keep him quiet again and at bay!...

* * *

One supposes Sergiolino was chosen to play Jesus Christ because of his age and his docile character.
He always had the victim role, a prime role it seemed!

He was aware of it being tailored for him but never in a million years he thought it was going to be for real, not 'just make belief' like they usually did!!

The older brother of Benito, Gennaro, always had a reputation of behaving like a natural leader, a figure of harsh and powerful authority. The children accepted and never argued about that. Furthermore, it was a mighty handy excuse to have him under one's belt if someone had to be blamed if things went badly out of hand...

After a long walk through the garden "We tied Sergiolino to an ancient old olive tree", Gennaro said ever so proudly with a generous smile, "and we whipped him very very hard because he was very very naughty. And he got all black and blue cause we bruised him so much". Gennnaro going overboard as his usual said laughing and victoriously. "I didn't hyphenated him", said the little boy shaking his head vigorously in all directions", "I didn't, because it was Maria Madelena's brother and she never doesn't give any spankings"

"I swear it's the truth!" he said insistently, convincing himself also as much as he could, with his round eyes that were nearly coming out of their sockets.

Sometimes the children can be so irrevocably cruel! One has to accept it is just like that are there no two ways about it...

Nevertheless, one could also see on the other side of the coin; he was so adorable looking at his performance with such his irresistible child charm and innocence, taking a plunge at the floor with his face turning rapidly dark pink revealing that he was lying...

"We runned very very fast and very very far because he was shouting so loud and he scared us and grownups could of hear him too!"

He was in so much pain and couldn't run anywhere poor kid! remember? he was still attached to the tree!

* * *

They also knew about the terrible story of Jesus so well because the film of his tragic life was shown every year without failure during. Easter time at the local village open air cinema parlour owned by Fiorella's father.

Fully packed with all the villagers, some gripping on the walls, trees and bushes, some over the fence with plenty of handkerchiefs of different sizes, usually white. The audience were kept in suspension ready to oblige all the tear jerking, keen audience with their bulging eyes full of tears of sorrow and pain prepared to weep instantly on command *because of* unbearable cruel and sad scenes happening throughout the film...
It lasted from the word GO to the words THE END.

Although the public knew the story by heart, back to front, inside out, they knew each move, each whisper, all the words and sentences! This happened EVERY year without failure!

Never THE END changed to a more compassionate one!...it would never end with '...and they lived happily ever after' so the crowd could walk out without feeling guilty, with wide smiles and OUFS sounds of relief.

The small children didn't 'get it' so they were less affected...Their 'attention span' didn't last long enough to correctly register the abysmal tragedy of what was going on and were instead playing innocently on and off before getting back to the screen time to time...

* * *

There was Sergio, he was gentle and kind, a 'good soul', and 'the wise'. He was the gang's oldest boy and had almost reached the age to be promoted to the "Adults

Forever". The group of course without entirely noticing this.

The Children mixed up the themes of playing during the day and with night fairy tales recounted by Mother or Father or more often by Sergilino, before going to sleep. He always kept a vigilant Eagle's eye on the Children so that nothing bad would happen to them. He was like their personal guardian Angel. Then he would walk back to his home on the edge of the Village.

* * *

They never lied; they had been well warned not to, and learnt their lesson for good from Pinocchio's story, who was punished for telling lies, by having his nose transformed to an exceptionally long, blushing red snout. No child was willing and prepared to run the risk of being exposed to such shame.

***

If someone called you an 'asino', (donkey) which means being stupid or lazy, it would mean they were the unfortunate village's idiot. Oh! Oh! boy were you in very deep trouble with everyone on site, including also this time with God and his potential varied punishments.

It was a bad bad ore deal! no one wanted to be in such horrifying and humiliating ore deal!

***

There existed some very very nasty children suffering of a type of 'children's hysteria'.

The trembling tormented terrified poor idiot child victim would be chased by those evil children throughout the village some of them holding sticks for beating while insulting and tormenting the youngster along this brutal, ruthless heartless hunt and hysterically nasty children procession.

Some adults were trying to contain this horrific and preposterous situation of cruel hunt but barely could, the children were so wild!

Fortunately, this event only happened once when the Children lived in Paradise.

It was a like a freak exceptionally rare event. Once in a blue moon you might say! Yet another warning that evil is always promptly lurking ready to strike.

* * *

According to the church establishment and to religion, it was vigorously and eminently important for the church to have permanently in the children's minds ... to be the focal point of the Children's upbringing which automatically englobed religion.

***

Also Sundays was the most significant day of the week and every week...for the church, not the children!...

The children had to dress up with their Sunday best clothes to go to mass and blend in with the Villagers traditions so to be genially approved and accepted by the Village.

Otherwise it would naturally be yet again an added of the already long list of mortal sins for 'unattendance to church', one supposes!'

They've must have done so many mortal sins one over the years! even the ones they did without willingly knowing! There was no hope for them one would say!

It was the weekly theatrical village priest show to boost to up his ego to the maximum capacity for seven days, until the reoccurring Sunday...

He did dramatic and threatening speeches with elaborated gestures on a high stage to keep his followers on the 'right path'!

It wasn't at all pleasant for children to go to Church and their natural short attention spell!

A painful every 7th day torture to stay quiet and not fidget for such a long time, and never understanding what the hell was being discussed about! Oh! what a huge sigh of relief when every time it but is was still finally all ended!

That still was a small price to live in Paradise, it's a mighty very good deal!

* * *

At last, they could go and play all over again before their traditional Sunday lunch as always.

It was invariably roast chicken with roast potatoes and a nice dessert, usually a chocolate one.

After the meal, the Parents would always drink exquisite coffee on the hot sunny patio, under the shade of a big umbrella ('ombrellone').

When the father finished this ritual nectar drink, his cup faithfully swiftly disappeared under the table for the little boy to have the exclusivity and the privilege to the last three sips of this nectar and savour at great length with honour, absolute respect this succulent delight!

It was supposed to be a grave ceremony state secret solely between the father and himself! It was a grand secret that unified father and son!

Little did he suspect that everybody silently knew about this except the little boy...

***

CARNIVAL

Where everything halted, froze, nobody home!
Every year the most important event of the Island was held, the focal point: the CARNIVAL (CARNEVALE), when everything halted and froze!

Everybody was very excited for this yearly event. The people prepared for it throughout the year with utter devoutness, dedication, zeal, keenness and fervour, starting from the day after the end of the previous carnival. It was exclusive, there was absolutely nothing else in the world that mattered. NOTHING...

All the Islanders gathered in the square near the sea of the Island's main Town. The scenery of the background was composed of a bay where every year a huge procession took place in front of the picturesque décor. There was an imposing high and dark castle, sitting in shallow sea and barely connected to the Island by a narrow strip of land. One could easily imagine living in a faraway century.

Late in the night, a long display of artistically dressed boats paraded in the bay, exhibiting incredibly varied and imaginative scenes, each one more spectacular than the other. The most impressive boat won a prize. The whole crowd, filled with admiration, would cheer loudly and profusely.

To top up the festivities, a specialist from the mainland prepared beforehand and ignited a famous Fireworks display from the illuminated castle. It lasted so long one could think it would never stop. At the end, the delighted public would loudly cheer abundantly for a long time once more.

All the children were in carnival costumes, made months before by their creative mothers. Every year they were extremely diverse and imaginative, all colours and topics, different shapes and materials.

The Crowd was happy and dense. There was only pure joy! The Children had sparklers lit up for them by the adults and cotton wool candy gave them sticky beards for a while.

The sky was lit up with a full display of near or far stars and there were drums, some made spontaneously from glasses or different lengths sticks or anything going, and music played, echoing from everywhere.

There were magicians blowing fire out of their mouths high up into the sky like dragons would do and men with coloured turbans round their heads, hypnotically lifting snakes by the sound of their flute. There were acrobats, jugglers, storytellers, dancers, contortionists, what else?

The people were eating, drinking, singing and bouncing - some in couples, some in a group - from the rhythm of the loudly performed music.

Everything was spinning with joy and excitement, with big shooting stars or

fluorescent necklaces that one could buy everywhere, shining heaps in the night.
After hours of such liveliness, gradually, the volume wandering in the sky decreased. The electrifying energy cooled down and became calmer then peaceful, then silent.

The little Girl and the little Boy returned home at dawn in an open three-wheeled scooter (motorino), totally exhausted, sucking their thumbs, sleeping on their Parents shoulders, before ending up in their cozy welcoming beds, still full of the images and immense splendour they'd just been experiencing.

* * *

The Children lived joyfully their 'Paradise years' and had a lot more adventures yet to be told.

A few years later, though they were still children some children started going to primary school! It happened in the highest peak of the village hill where sat the old run-down castle to the great pride of the villagers. The learning quarters happened on the safe part of the old castle where one could view down to the sea, opposing the very crumbling side of the castle. All the mothers and women like Commara Marguerita handled the daily walk to accompany the children up the hill, with the complementary joyful sounds of laughter, encouragement, reassuring and a whole range of dynamic sounds to accompany this mainly joyful group.

* * *

The little boy was eager to learn, he didn't want to miss out on anything. Since the first time in his life he had heard about 'the donkeys and children' saga he was always so so worried! and at all times was very concerned and feared becoming donkey (asino) himself if he might fail not going to be vigilant enough, which equalled 'being stupid'.

If someone called you an 'asino', boy you were in deep trouble with everyone on site! An enormous no no for him.

Sometimes the little Boy used to cry profusely about this when he felt deeply sad. He was then inconsolable, especially when he was very tired or when a donkey started to brey in his dreams or for real.

His heart rate went even sky high, and he cried even harder...

Later he was very troubled and most concerned of how some grownups can manage to be able to completely distort the truth to justify and believe in their lies, to the extent they commit the sacrilegious crime of also polluting the cosmos?!&'*

* * *

The Teacher was very strict but at the same time so very nice.

She was a real special teacher...

She was as short as the children and fat, she resembled a rounded cube or barrel, same width front or side.

In addition, she was invaded by warts with hairs covering her face, neck, all over.
One couldn't decide if it was a she or a he but was very nice.

But when she started talking or singing one melted in a cocoon of reassurance and complete confidence and the negative description from people disappeared in thin air. Her voice and her reassuring tone was eternally soothing.

Whatever she/he was she/he showed the little boy how to write for the first time ever.

She explained to the little Boy for the first time ever how to tackle the new experience of writing. He was extremely distressed because when he reached the end of the line, he didn't have the slightest clue what to do next and totally panicked!

"You simply start again on the next line", said the teacher explaining how to pursue forward with such a reassuring voice.

What a discovery!

He never distressed or panicked again for anything...

That day he also learned an added plus: "always to be 'positive in life" and he was from ever onwards!...

***

The little Boy remained ecstatic for the rest of the week!

After school, he marched triumphantly throughout the Village like a great hero, with a baton in his hand, swinging it from left to right and up and down to an imaginary music, hearing the huge illusory applause from the crowd.

***

There was a beautiful young girl who came every day to the Children's home to do the cleaning, the cooking and taking care of the Children. Her name was Marguerita like the flower rose.

She was like a second mother to them; they adored her, and she adored the Children. She was devoted to them as if they were her own.

She married Luca for love. Sadly, she was unable to have Children of her own. Rossetta and Tonino became the Children's God Parents later on. The Children called her, God Mother Marguerita (Commara Marguerita).

She despaired at their appalling eating habits. She always used to say: "with you two it's always the same, 'potatoes and meat' one day and 'meat and potatoes' the next day," shaking her head in desperation.

The Children didn't like fish very much, it smelled too fishy, and 'this' was too sour, and 'that' too savoury, and 'that' too soft, and 'this' too hard.

***

Rarely there was running water in the houses, so Giuseppe the fisherman, brought fresh water to the Children's house every morning from the public well, up the hill called "il Soccorso".

There were a lot of men called Giuseppe. To distinguish them, one added their profession after their name.

Giuseppe-the-fisherman also brought water to Giuseppe-the-old-carpenter; he was so old! He was totally out of action. He could hardly stand up or walk and was nearly blind, with thick glasses, as thick as handmade bottle bottoms. They were so thick, mamma mia! (my goodness!)

He needed help and all the Villagers were happy to oblige, cooking food, cleaning, fetching water... His modest bedroom was his old carpentry workshop.

He lived next door to Marguerita, who also occupied a very modest narrow house with her numerous family members. The home was so tiny, noisy and crowded, that one wondered if they took turns to sleep. And what did they do when it rained? Who knows!

Later they added up another floor with two other bedrooms to earn extra money from the rare 'modest' tourist...

* * *

There was no television, and if one needed to telephone it was an everlasting traumatising performance!

Telephoning or Telegrams, although intolerably expensive, were the best option for contacting someone urgently,

To achieve that it was an expedition of patience and sheer solid determination to go to the main post office to the Capital of the island where the yearly Carnival takes place remember?

Very often the line of the telephone was incredibly crackly.

Sometimes one couldn't hear or guess what the other party was saying, and one had to shout at full lungs hoping that somebody could hear.

And a lot of the crowds in the post office had their hands covering their ears, being deafened by all the shouting going on.

It took all day for this tedious operation and return home late at night washed out. No wonder this experience was only reserved for emergencies or sadists!

* * *

The Socorsso was famous to be an attractive focal point in Town. There was a modest garden covered with common red tiles with some exotic plants with no shade available. It was so beautiful because it was so modest. At the end of the piazza there was a precious and modest little Church clinging at the edge of the sea... It was a favourite place to enjoy plenty of activities. Also, the park was comfortably large enough for children to learn how to cycle for the first time and proudly cycle safely. It involved of course without saying a lot of pride, tears, damaged knees as well as teeth.

* * *

There was Fabio, innocently so beautiful. He couldn't come and play and join and fool around very often with the group.

Usually, he was covered with white flower contrasting with his striking big glittering dark black eyes to die for; they were like flickering butterflies, you could nearly become hypnotised by them.

Fabio helped his father, the baker, to make the daily bread for the Village.
The two Children went there sometimes to visit him and pretended to bake in what seemed a huge bakery.

They made elaborate cake mixtures which always failed miserably. At the end went rapidly like glue and hardened incredibly quickly. They became as solid as stone and invariably ended up with a bang in the bin. After which, they would unavoidably go to 'Bar Maria' for 'nice creams' to console themselves and get over their lamentable flop.

* * *

And there was Fiorella, whose father owned the outdoor movie parlour, and her awfully sour, bossy, ugly mother.

Fiorella's mother had a shop with shelves on every wall, ready to collapse at any moment, with a multitude of goods of all kinds to sell or fall to the ground. It was dangerous! It's true to say, if the shelves ever fell, one could seriously risk being buried alive! Fiorella was so serious she never participated in recreations; she never had any, she wasn't allowed to.

She had to work for her mother all the time and she rarely revealed a happy smile to anyone! She liked serious conversations or alternatively, to escape she liked reading every moment she could. She frowned a lot, while her mother was yelling incessantly at her, like a hyena, to come to serve and sell to the eventual tourist customers in the shop.

***

Then, one day, huge threatening dark clouds descended on the Island! It was time to be torn away from this idyllic location. For certain it was the end of Paradise! Without noticing it they were starting to become grownups after all.

Their Parents announced one day: "The Children need proper schooling and culture". They were moved abroad a couple of months after that sentence was pronounced, in Autumn it was, to an oppressive, humid town in northern France. That place had nothing to do with HEAVEN, Ohhh no!

It was so traumatising, the Children were startled, in total disbelief. But it was the same tariff would one like it or not hence they had no other choice than to 'chin up' have a "stiff upper lip" and be resigned. They had to get used to it, they were condemned, because nothing could be done in the world that existed to solve and undo this tragic wretched omen.

* * *

The days in winter were dark, cold and so unwelcome. There were many more rainy days than sunny ones.

"Heaven, where have you gone?" they cried distressfully without the hope of a nearby echo in site.

* * *

The children had no time for playing with sticks or anything going. They became separated in different classrooms depending on their age. 15 minutes break in the morning, the same in the afternoon.

The court yards were separated from small children to even smaller ones! Thus the separation of children became deeper and even more traumatising than before...

There was also the dreaded homework to do after school for the next day or next week.

The days in winter were dark, cold so uninviting. There was a lot more rainy days than sunny ones.

Heaven where are you gone, they cried distressfully still without an echo in site! Had they really committed another mortal sin?

Surely, they would of remembered?
Religion was hammered so constantly in their heads!
It was an integral part of their upbringing after all!...

What such bad thing have we done to deserve this they repeatedly exclaimed???

Paradise had vanished from planet Earth without a warning! Incinerated! Evaporated!
POUF! like the piercing of a big soap bubble...

* * *

The Children kept on speaking their funny English with their mother, but their main language was now French, which they spoke with their Father and at school. However, they always maintained their Italian when they spoke to each other, especially when they were playing, quibbling or swapping secrets!

They still remembered their funny English, which became later a little more polished at school.

But the 'Chicken on Sunday treat' was still faithfully on the menu. Yippee! It was also served on special occasions too, so the

Children counted the days when the next special occasion would arrive...

* * *

After the children left Paradise Island the Children finally met 'Granny' for the first time. She was so old; she came from nearly two centuries ago.

She was just a traditional Granny, very frail and ancient to the children's eyes; her voice was so faint one could barely understand what she was saying. One could easily hear a pin drop before perceiving her inaudible weak voice.
When she expressed discontent or disapproval, she only had to clap her hands once and all was immediately back to order. The times when the Children went to see her, there was always a new toy waiting for them in the bed. They considered her good, generous and very welcoming. She always

had a joyful laugh to express how amused she was which was quite often.

Granny regularly gave some money to the Children's father to help the family going. She was rich, stinking rich to our eyes!
She came from that breed, where there was a huge divide from rich and poor and it was blatantly outrageous. The poor were very poor and where the staff usually lived for life in the kitchen quarters owned by whoever they were serving.

Granny was aware to be an 'upper class', and of the wrong doings or the right doings!
That's the way it was, it never occurred to anyone to question it, especially the rich one supposes!

Being young the Children weren't aware she wasn't as rich anymore. Nonetheless

Granny continued living very comfortably and wasn't short of anything...

Her deceased husband had diligently left her a generous pension that still allowed her to have a helper every day to help her for the chores in her smart generous house.

* * *

The years passed... slowly... very slowly.
One didn't notice at first that the heavenly Paradise Island was becoming famous. Over the years a jungle of Luxury hotels, expensive posh restaurants multiplied, and dancing clubs flared up very rapidly in abundance. Numerous beaches became exclusive to privileged prestigious hotels Owners or Companies, Holiday resorts, mud baths, and private millionaires.

Admittedly in the same time slums at the edge of the Village were slowly disappearing.

They were no more Golden beaches and swimming with the fish and the amazingly abundant, beautiful shells similar to the delicious past.

They became extinct due to pollution.

One felt vehemently imposed and forcefully resigned to embrace the la-di-da buildings, yachts and speed boats full of shining diesel floating on the surface on the sea zooming plentifully with no regard for others and nature, except themselves.

A new imposing modern pier was built, much bigger, wider and longer, with an intruding harbour to receive the daily floods of tourists. The old, abandoned pier became so offensively out of proportion by now with the already disfigured Village.

They even built a road through the beach! The huge rock part of the picture of the idyllic beach, was blown up and buried rock under a newly built road. It was cut through under the sacred church to come out on the other side of the hill. The beach, of course, was destroyed in the process. The natives used to sit all around the huge rock looking like a docile playful whale, whilst the children were playing all sorts of fun games on it! Another added sad disappearance...

The fishermen packed up and sold their gear. There was no more fishing, just tour-boats which made more money. The fishing was done by larger boats, 'trawlers', which had to go further out to sea to find fish. There was none left nearer the shore.

The beautiful spectacle of the great variety and rich colours of corals surrounding the Island, which were once profuse, was destroyed. The future generations will be deprived from such magical nature.

The older Islanders spoke daily about the past, with heavy, sad eyes and immense nostalgia. "We were poorer, perhaps, but so much more jovial in those old happy days!" looking back down onto memory lane.

The fishing nets survived by being recycled for decoration purposes. They were destined to be cut and hung to embellish the naked walls of those beautiful natural arches of the dead fishing depots on the beach. They became partly attached to the new Port. They were also sold elsewhere, be it by individuals, markets, souvenir shops, to the never-ending supply of tourists.

Life like before didn't exist anymore, that's for sure.

* * *

The children used to be so very enthusiastic by merely playing with a stick and their extraordinary inventive imagination. It could incite them to play with it all day and even perhaps until the next day and the next one also...!

* * *

Nearly all the Children of the Village, by this time grown-ups with numerous babies, getting fatter and fatter every year, still remained in the Village, doing jobs for rich people that were holding and pulling out bundles of large banknotes, replaced, much much later on, by countless plastic payment cards.

* * *

Benito and Gennaro took over their retired father's practice and became the Village new lawyers. They were very clever, fierce, powerful and efficient. They had a significant say in what had to be done for the benefit of the Village and the Island. No one would have dared to contradict them.

Fabio continued in his father's footsteps and carried on working in the bakery, still covered with white flower contrasting with those exceptional big, shimmering, hypnotic, shiny black eyes. He was famous for supplying hotels with a delicious wide variety of exclusive new pastries and breads of all kinds.

Sergiolino was the owner of an 'ice cream' parlour. Actually, it was his jealous and bossy wife that owned it. Unfortunately, and regrettably, there would be no more 'nice creams' for him ever again.

Ilario became an important hotel manager for the rich. He never had time for anyone or anything, but always had an attractive smile for his customers especially the richest ones and was always extremely stressed out.

Benvenuto's Deli ('Salumeria') was sold to another native family; it had more varieties of delicacies to sell to the tourists.

'Bar Maria' didn't move, but there was a new modern fountain in the middle of the square that changed all the dynamics of the old 'Piazza'.

There was one exception to the rule though: Fiorella, who landed on the mainland, never came back to the Island, never married and became a highly appreciated and respected doctor!

***

The laundry was washed by washing women gathered at the outdoor washing parlour next to the Church while happily continuously chatting laughing, dancing...

It was a women's liberation when finally, their washing was replaced by washing machines, vacuum cleaners and many other useful utensils of that kind appeared quite a few years later. Toys were replaced by plastic one's and much later by numerous computer games...

It is so sad that one can never change the alterations of time.

The little Girl learned a lot by reading books. She was a real sponge for absorbing knowledge.

She became very intellectual. Now a young woman, she settled down in another country far from Paradise which eventually became a long-lasting memory. She worked and was enormously fulfilled as a professor in her town, at a World-renowned University.

She is well-respected and very much loved and appreciated for her great knowledge and devotion she brought to her students. She still lives there to this very day...

While the little Boy was more about talking and doing...

◊ THE ATYPICAL WAY ◊

...The little boy, now a young man, was very keen for adventures!
Judges could of easily defined him as being "unconventional".

Very early on he made different choices of living - in an atypical way, naturally!

As for traditional people, 'breaking the rules' can be very irritating.

It's like throwing a pebble into a pond where people could only notice its stagnant stillness getting disturbed. Rather than marvel at the look of the shimmering ripple full of glitter thanks to just such a tiny stone...

He just went trotting and gently strolling through life, living very contently in his own unique way.

He never managed to figure how grammatical rules functioned and why they existed. What they were for, except to distressingly muddle up brains!!! Though it was said being of mega importance!

For him it was all just about phonetics and feelings if it sounded right or wrong. It was all too complicated it gave him severe headaches and vertigo.

To be fair, he really did make serious attempts to understand those numerous rules but his continuous failure... nearly killed him.

And after a long time of despairing to behave like the norm, he finally found his own recipe.

He was not able to conduct himself otherwise. Why worth worrying? there is so much awaiting to learn, to discover, to marvel!

He could only function with phonetics and feelings. It became part of his language collection. Until this day he had never managed to master any languages quite together and had a stranger's accent in every one of them.

It was OK not to know correctly all the languages.

He ended up in Spain and, shortly after, he was able to eventually 'espekka a bitta of Espanish'.

He was a loner for several years but certainly never felt lonely. It was a good period, it made him wiser and stronger, more mature and it toughened up his character, his being!

He became a 'Jack of all trades' and was an excellent one too.

A few years later, he met an exquisitely nice girl who was in the same situation as him.

They were so excited to have found each other, they ran out of words the first time they met... Very gradually they started murmuring together like cats do to express their great delight.

They married a few moons later in expected full extravagancy.

The couple went to Russia, then Brazil and eventually, they glided all around the globe.

They still are together until today...

By choosing such a unique learning ground they joyfully merely carried on speaking in their "personalised manner".

It was their choice of school, the school of life, so be it!! They disconcerted people with their unusual behaviour since they were so dissimilar to others.

There were those who were irritated or even hated them. They troubled people because they weren't the norm, they were a misfit for society, they didn't fit the picture!

Some of them believed they were maybe mentally retarded or at least quite stupid, not quite there!

And to think that there are so many of them that can't even discern between "being ignorant" or "stupid!"

One wonders... surely some might have of been jealous?

Some conditioned people don't allow others to be different, it disturbs the run of their 'habits', of 'tradition', 'the way one does...'!

Though sometimes it would be upsetting, deep down they really didn't care!

They decided a long time ago that there's nothing wrong to be ignorant, after all we all are to a certain degree. There's so much to learn, no one could ever learn it all anyway!

It was their choice of school, the school of life, so be it!! They disconcerted people with their unusual behaviour since they were so dissimilar to others.

There were those who were irritated or even hated them.

They knew they were unusual 'and a little bit ignorant but they powerfully felt their life was so much richer than those 'criticisers' and at the end of the day they would have the last laugh.

For them aggressive people were something that was the least of their problems.

Their main drive was to encounter as many people of all countries and learn from them as much as they could.

To communicate, they employed a variety of means, like creative cooking with art, carefully mixing different foods, spices, and ingredients to achieve mouth-watering, scrumptious, yummy dishes. The languages they eventually learned were like a bundle of entangled spaghettis, sprinkled with noises of German he once was obliged to learn at school The cooking was so inspirational, so thrilling!
The diversity range of expressions they had recourse for any situation or events became vast.

They would add chosen words from the locals, learned through their travels, appropriate for the circumstance.

They had a wild imagination and prolific creativity and invented many words, enabling them to express what they wanted to say as precisely as they could of those so many everlasting feelings. Needless to say, quite a few words were even involved with Magic!

Imitations of expressions and animal noises, with all kinds of different shapes and grimaces, music, singing and dancing, smiling, laughing, playing, joking, performing music, grinning and added a few more whisks of flavours, just like chefs do, tasting their dishes before serving them.

This type of existence stimulated, invigorated and enthused them, they felt so totally alive!

Their verbal cooking was so inspirational, so thrilling; other choices of living were inexistent!

The cherry on the cake was when they encountered people of the same kind, that were bi tri or more lingual. Boy did they have loads of fun playing with their tongues!

About Nicole d'Altena

Writing is what keeps Nicole ticking!

She was born into an Anglo-Belgian family in the U.S.A.. Shortly after, Nicole's nomadic life in Europe started in Italy. Having travelled and lived in too many countries to mention, she finally settled in Cornwall UK for over 40 years.

Her stories rest on her recollection of numerous encounters and experiences acquired during her life and travels, witnessing and sharing a wide range of situations. She offers plenty of fiction mixed with day and night dreams and memories, as well as expressing imagination in an unusual way. Each story is quite unique in its own original way. There is absolutely no formula.

She hopes to impart a way of seeing life in a constructive, positive and dynamic way with its abundant optimistic potential: life can be very enjoyable sometimes, even if on occasions she must object and denounce flaws. That is her basic philosophy.

The book has been now translated in Italian, in Spanish and in French and will be commercialized later on in those languages. It also will be offered to many Children's Charities.

Nicole wishes that this book will entice all readers, make them simile, laugh and most importantly have a lot of enjoyment from them. Share and enjoy! Nicole

DESTINITY